WISHBONE

For Marc, who buried the first bone. My love, Neen JB

For Minnie KN

The ABC 'Wave' device and the 'ABC For Kids' device are trademarks of the Australian Broadcasting Corporation and are used under licence by HarperCollins*Publishers* Australia.

First published in 2002 by ABC Books for the
AUSTRALIAN BROADCASTING CORPORATION.
Reprinted by HarperCollins*Publishers* Australia Pty Limited
ABN 36 009 913 517
harpercollins.com.au

Copyright © text Janeen Brian 2002
Copyright © illustrations Kilmeny Niland 2002

The rights of Janeen Brian and Kilmeny Niland to be identified as the author and illustrator of this work have been asserted in accordance with the *Copyright Amendment (Moral Rights) Act 2000*.

This work is copyright. Apart from any use as permitted under the *Copyright Act 1968*, no part may be reproduced, copied, scanned, stored in a retrieval system, recorded, or transmitted, in any form or by any means, without the prior written permission of the publisher.

HarperCollins*Publishers*
25 Ryde Road, Pymble, Sydney, NSW 2073, Australia
31 View Road, Glenfield, Auckland 0627, New Zealand
A 53, Sector 57, Noida, UP, India
77–85 Fulham Palace Road, London W6 8JB, United Kingdom
2 Bloor Street East, 20th floor, Toronto, Ontario M4W 1A8, Canada
10 East 53rd Street, New York NY 10022, USA

National Library of Australia
Cataloguing-in-Publication entry
Brian, Janeen, 1948— .
Wishbone.
ISBN 9780 7333 09748 Hardback.
ISBN 9780 7333 11161 Paperback.
1. Dogs — Juvenile fiction. I. Niland, Kilmeny. II. Australian Broadcasting Corporation. III. Title.
A823.3

Set in ITC Giovanni Book 20/27
Designed by Monkeyfish
The illustrations for this book were painted with watercolours
Colour reproduction by Graphic Print Group, Adelaide
Printed and bound in China by RR Donnelley on 128gsm matt art

6 5 4 3   11 12 13

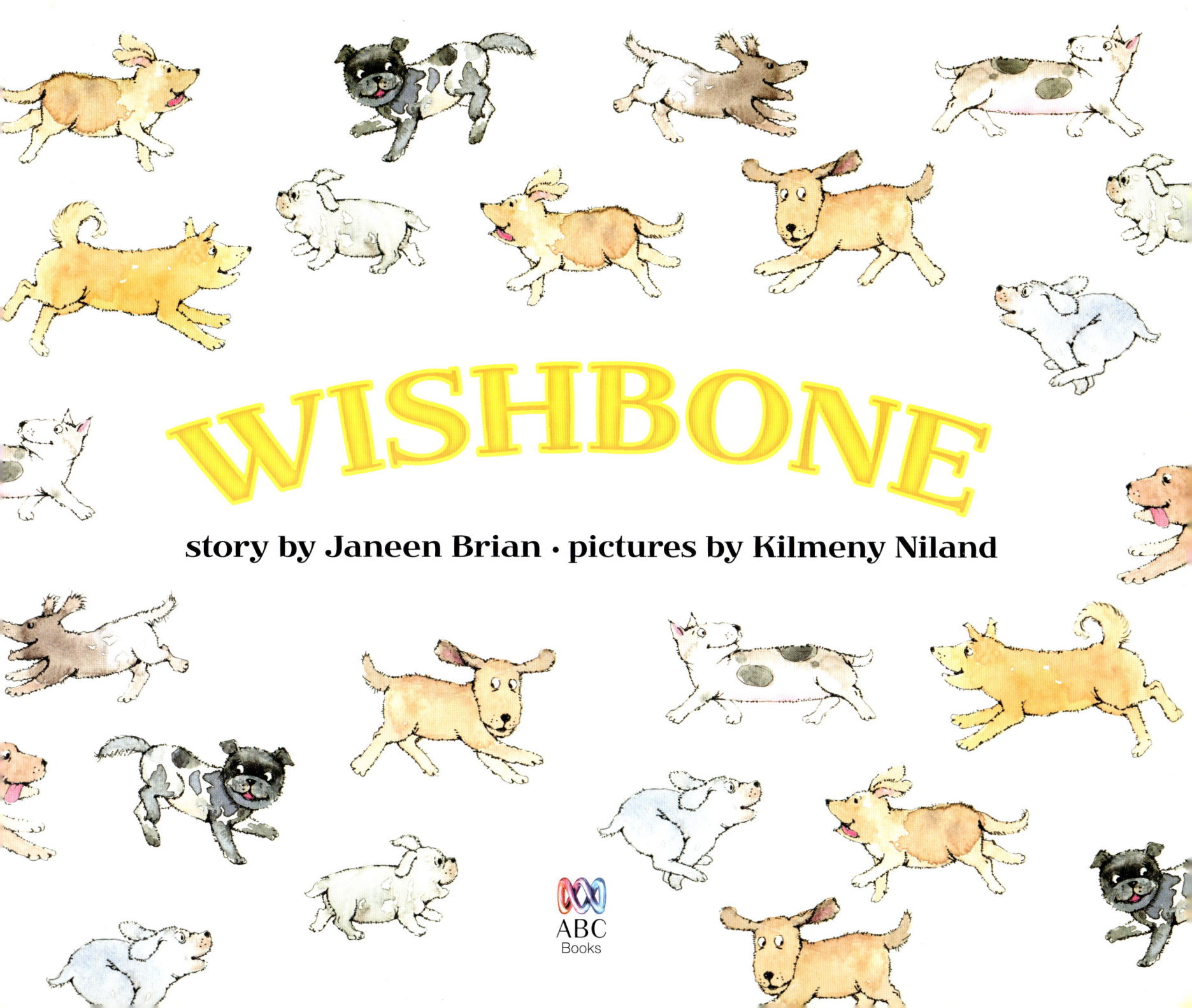

WISHBONE

story by Janeen Brian · pictures by Kilmeny Niland

ABC Books

Henry wanted a dog.

He wanted a little rough-and-tumble dog with feathery ears and eyes as black as licorice.

Or a happy-go-lucky dog that splashed in puddles on wet, muddy days.

Or a roly-poly dog that loved to have its tummy tickled.

But Henry's mum said a dog would be too lonely on its own while she was at work and Henry was at school.

So every afternoon, Henry
went next-door to play
with Mr Perry's dog.
Wagger had soft, fluffy ears,
a long, swishy tail —
and lots of old doggy bones
to chew!

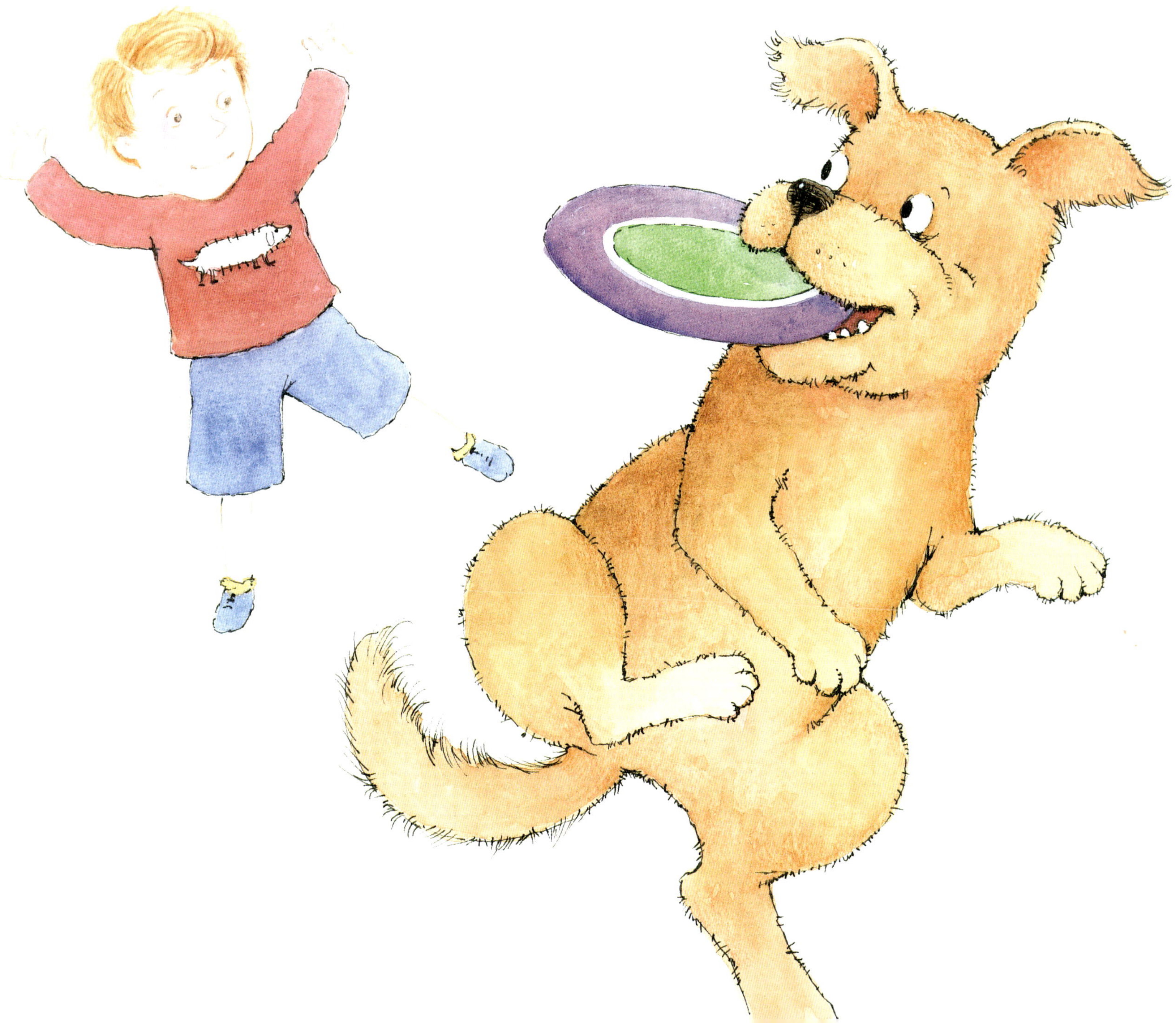

When it was time to go home,
Henry always hugged Wagger and
said, "I like you, Wagger,
but I *wish* I had a dog of my own."

One afternoon,
Wagger dropped a bone
at Henry's feet.

"For me?" said Henry,
picking it up.
"Thanks, Wagger,
but I don't have a dog
to give it to."

Henry looked at
the bone. It was a *real*
dog bone. Maybe he could
keep it and pretend he had
a *real* dog! He shoved the
bone into his pocket
and gave Wagger a hug.

When Henry went home,
his mum said,
"Come and help me plant
these beans, Henry."
She showed him how to
scoop out the earth and
make a tiny hollow.
As she put each seed in
the ground, she said,
"I'll tell you a secret Henry.
Whenever I plant anything,
I make a wish.
And everything grows
just as I want."

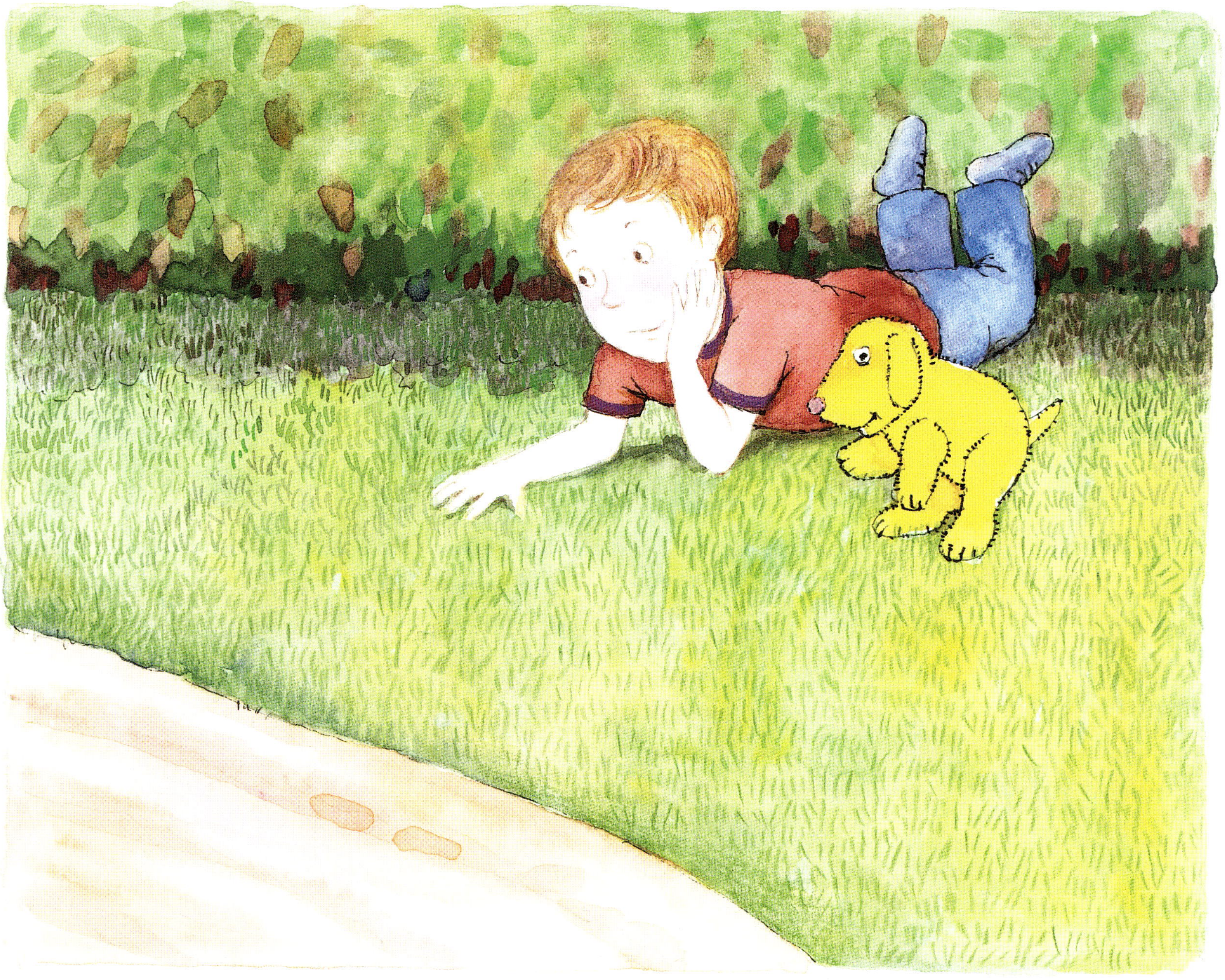

After his mum had gone inside,
Henry remembered the bone.
He took it out of his pocket.
He wasn't really sure he believed
in wishes, but …

Henry dug a hole and covered the bone. Then he wished very, very hard for a dog of his own.

That night, Henry thought about his wish. Perhaps it would come true …

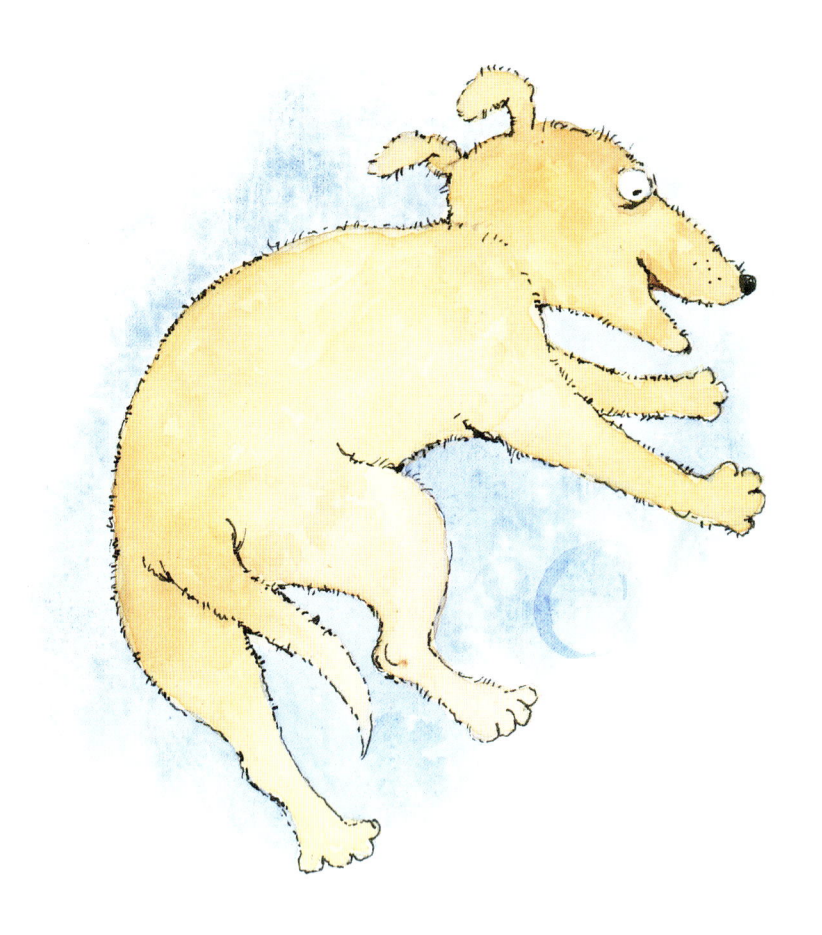

Perhaps his dog would be a helter-skelter dog that he had to chase whenever it was bath-time.

Or a large spotty dog that leapt and twisted to catch balls.

Or a trim sausage dog that strolled leisurely down the road.

The next afternoon, Henry watered the bean seeds and the bone — then he went next-door to play with Wagger.

He wanted to tell Wagger how he'd planted the bone and made a secret wish. But he didn't know if he should. It might spoil the wish.

Night after night,
Henry thought about his wish.

Perhaps his dog would be a short and perky dog,
the kind that dug holes at the beach and sent sand flying.

Or a furry dog with a faraway look in its eyes – a dog that chased butterflies and shadows.

Or a clever, clipped dog that jumped through the tyre swing in the backyard.

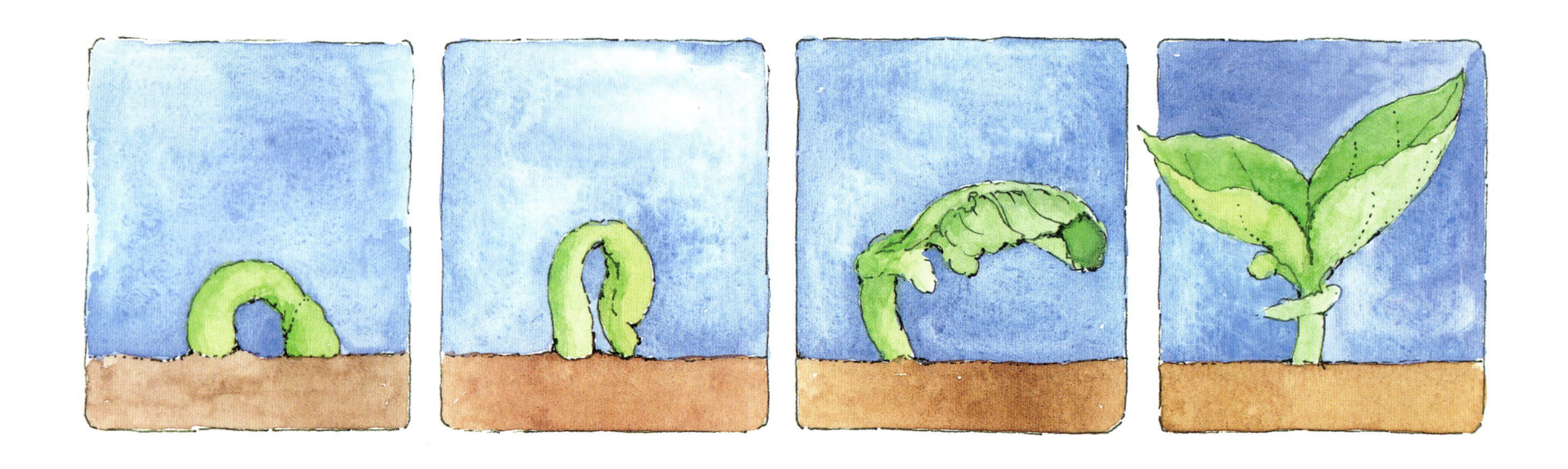

One afternoon, when Henry went to water
the garden, he saw tiny, curved beanstalks
pushing their way out of the earth.
He was pleased for his mum.
Her wish had come true.
Maybe his just needed more time …

He patted the soil
where he'd buried the bone,
then went next-door
to visit Wagger. But this
time, Henry didn't feel
much like playing.

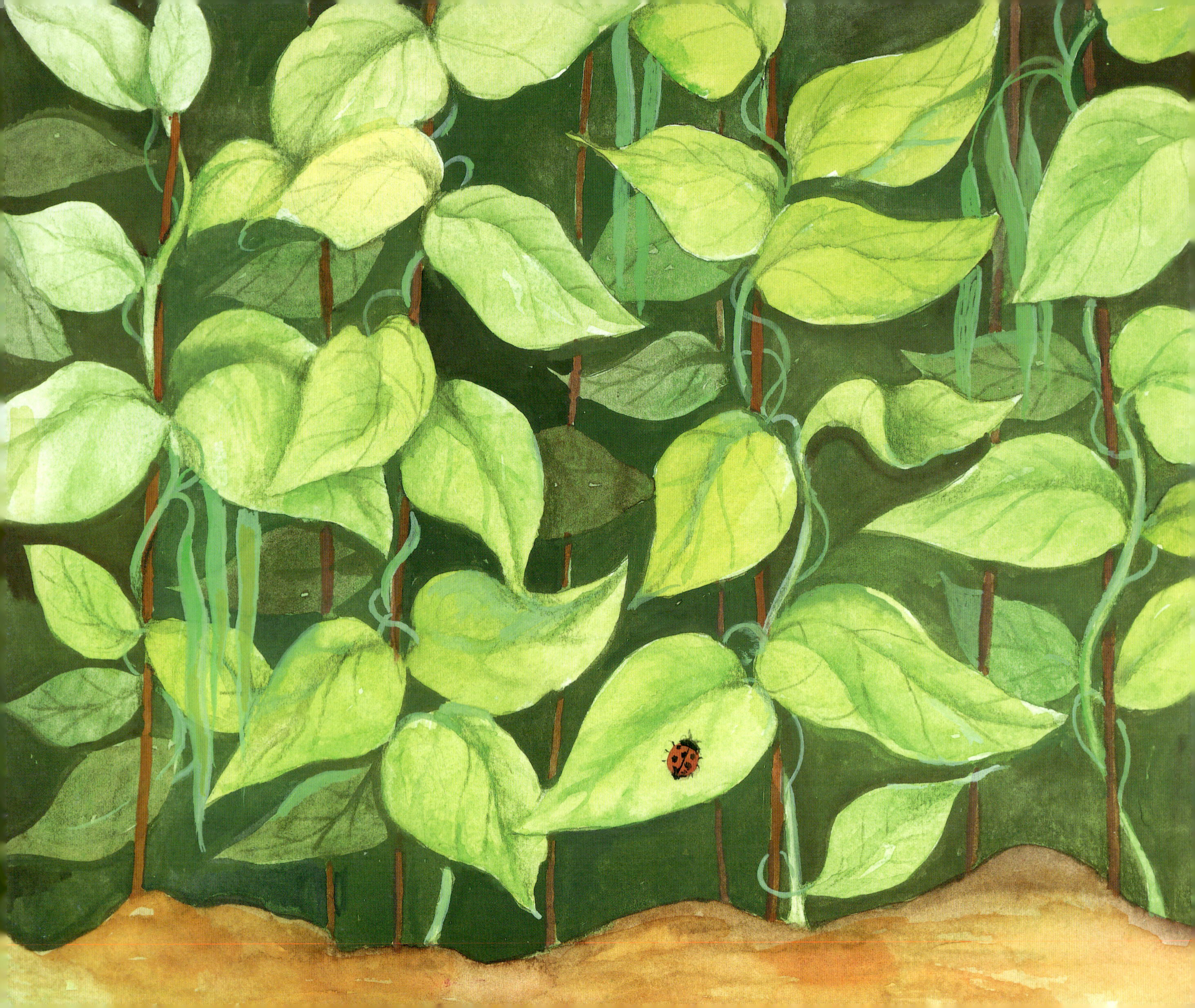

Days passed and the bean plants
grew tall and green and rambly.
But the place where Henry had
planted the bone stayed brown and bare.

Then one morning, Henry heard
a small, excited bark.
He peeped outside. His heart thumped,
for there by the bean patch,
with a bone in its mouth, was a dog.
A little rough-and-tumble dog
with feathery ears and eyes as black as licorice.

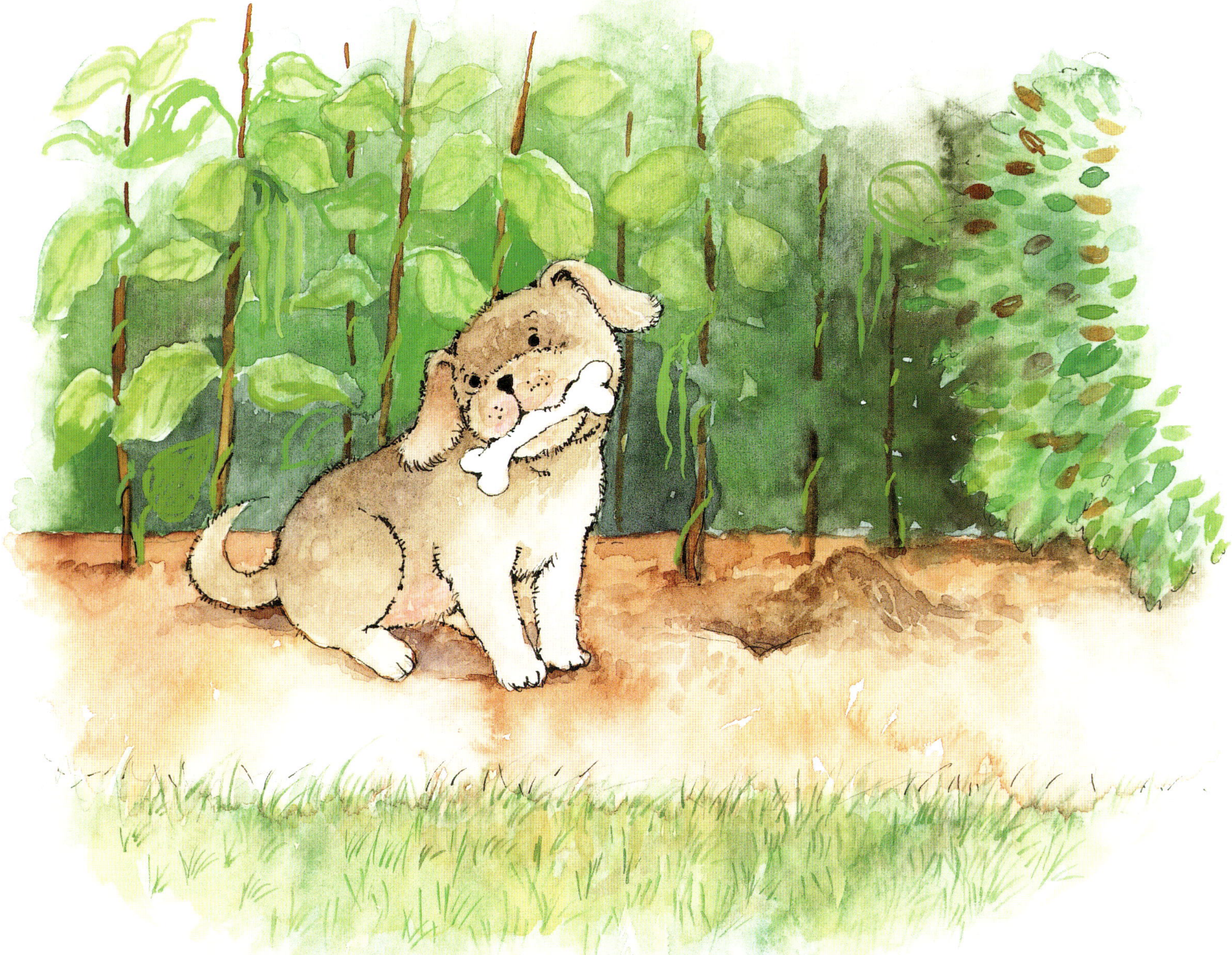

Henry knew just what to say to his dog …

HELLO WISHBONE!

Henry's mum asked around.
But no one claimed
the little dog.

Mr Perry offered to look after Wishbone during the day, and so Henry was allowed to keep him for his very own.

Henry loved Wishbone, but he never forgot
it had been Wagger who'd first given him the bone
and shown him that wishes can come true.